Ten Po
for a We

Candlestick Press

Published by:
Candlestick Press,
Diversity House, 72 Nottingham Road, Arnold, Nottingham NG5 6LF
www.candlestickpress.co.uk

Design and typesetting by Craig Twigg

Printed by Ratcliff & Roper Print Group, Nottinghamshire, UK

Selection and Introduction © Kathryn Bevis, 2023

Cover illustration © Hilke MacIntyre, 2023
http://hilke.macintyre-art.com

Candlestick Press monogram © Barbara Shaw, 2008

© Candlestick Press, 2023

ISBN 978 1 913627 23 2

Acknowledgements

The poems in this pamphlet are reprinted from the following books, all by
permission of the publishers listed unless stated otherwise. Every effort has been
made to trace the copyright holders of the poems published in this book. The
editor and publisher apologise if any material has been included without
permission, or without the appropriate acknowledgement, and would be glad to
be told of anyone who has not been consulted.

Thanks are due to all the copyright holders cited below for their kind permission.

Kathryn Bevis, *Flamingo* (Seren Books, 2022). Michael Donaghy, *Collected
Poems* (Picador, 2014). Sasha Dugdale, *Red House* (Oxford Poets, 2011) by
permission of Carcanet Press. Jane Hirshfield, *Come, Thief* (Bloodaxe Books,
2011) www.bloodaxebooks.com. William Meredith, Meredith, William. 'Tree
Marriage' from *Effort at Speech: New and Selected Poems*. Evanston:
TriQuarterly Books/Northwestern University Press, 1997, p.203. Alice Oswald,
The Thing in the Gap-Stone Stile (Faber & Faber, 2010). Clare Shaw, *Head On*
(Bloodaxe Books, 2012) www.bloodaxebooks.com. Li-Young Lee, *The
Undressing: Poems by Li-Young Lee*. Copyright © 2018 by Li-Young Lee. Used
by permission of WW Norton & Company, Inc.

All permissions cleared courtesy of Dr Suzanne Fairless-Aitken
c/o Swift Permissions swiftpermissions@gmail.com

Where poets are no longer living, their dates are given.

Introduction

Weddings are some of the most joyful days of our lives. Everything about them celebrates devotion and union, community and well-wishing: from the first invitations we slip into the postbox, the careful choosing of clothes, food and flowers, to the promises we make to one another, the exchange of rings and kisses, the dancing, feasting, cake-cutting and merrymaking with those who are closest to us. Above all, weddings allow us to declare our deepest and most abiding love towards our sweetheart before those who love us most. What could be finer than that?

In the ten poems I've chosen for you in this pamphlet, you'll discover poems which are passionate avowals of love, poems of blessing, poems which offer sage advice, and poems which promise a future built on love and togetherness.

In Sasha Dugdale's 'Blessing,' marital love is compared to a walled garden which contains within it: "Bluebell and harebell and comfrey and sage:/In the naming of love how sweet it grows...". In Alice Oswald's 'Wedding,' love is constantly shapeshifting, it is: "like a sail ... like a trumpeter, like luck ... like everything." Li-Young Lee and John Donne both choose to write about love's longings and fulfilments: "For love, all love of other sights controls,/And makes one little room an everywhere".

But these wedding poems don't simply wear rose-tinted glasses. They are not afraid to acknowledge and embrace what Jane Hirshfield describes as the "day and dark" of love, its "fierceness and tenderness." In Clare Shaw's exquisite poem, 'Vow,' the uncertainties and complexities involved in sharing a life together are greeted by a gaze that is as truthful as it is tender: "Love did not turn from hurt/or hard work./When lights failed, it did not switch off./When love had no road,/we willingly built it."

This little book is an immense oak table, glittering with candlelight, garlanded with flowers, and heaving with some of poetry's most brightly wrapped wedding gifts. I hope you enjoy each one as much as I do.

Kathryn Bevis

Wedding

From time to time our love is like a sail
and when the sail begins to alternate
from tack to tack, it's like a swallowtail
and when the swallow flies it's like a coat;
and if the coat is yours, it has a tear
like a wide mouth and when the mouth begins
to draw the wind, it's like a trumpeter
and when the trumpet blows, it blows like millions...
and this, my love, when millions come and go
beyond the need of us, is like a trick;
and when the trick begins, it's like a toe
tip-toeing on a rope, which is like luck;
and when the luck begins, it's like a wedding,
which is like love, which is like everything.

Alice Oswald

Vow

Say yes.
That word on your lips
is a kiss;
is a promise already made.
We made it.

Love did not turn from hurt
or hard work.
When lights failed, it did not switch off.
When love had no road,
we willingly built it.

We shouldered its stones
and its dirt. So thank god
there are days like this when it's easy.
When we open our mouths
and the words flood in.

Put the word of your hand
in mine.

We have learnt to hold to each other
when nothing was given by right;
how love will insist
with its ache; with its first painful
tug on the guts;

its snake in the nest of the ribs;
the bomb in the chest;
in the Y of the thighs; the red, red
red sun of it, rising.
How love must, at all costs,

be answered. We have answered
and so have a million before us
and each of their names is a vow.

So now I can tell you, quite simply
you are the house I will live in:

there is no good reason
to move. Good earth,
you are home, stone, sun,
all my countries. Vital to me
as the light. You are it

and I am asking.
Say yes.

Love opens a door
then slams it. It does.
It loses its touch and its looks.
But love needs its fury.
We have fought

and when times make it necessary,
we will again. When night draws in,
we won't forget
how once the streets ran wet with light
and love. Like blood. They will again.

But for now,
we make our promises gently.
This extraordinary day we have made.
Listen –
the birds in their ordinary heaven.

Tonight the sky will blaze
with stars. Today, my love,
rooms bloom with flowers.
Say yes.
The sky is ours.

Clare Shaw

I Loved You Before I Was Born

I loved you before I was born.
It doesn't make sense, I know.

I saw your eyes before I had eyes to see.
And I've lived longing
for your every look ever since.
That longing entered time as this body.
And the longing grew as this body waxed.
And the longing grows as this body wanes.
That longing will outlive this body.

I loved you before I was born.
It makes no sense, I know.

Long before eternity, I caught a glimpse
of your neck and shoulders, your ankles and toes.
And I've been lonely for you from that instant.
That loneliness appeared on earth as this body.
And my share of time has been nothing
but your name outrunning my ever saying it clearly.
Your face fleeing my ever
kissing it firmly once on the mouth.

In longing, I am most myself, rapt,
my lamp mortal, my light
hidden and singing.

I give you my blank heart.
Please write on it
what you wish.

Li-Young Lee

The Good-Morrow

I wonder, by my troth, what thou and I
Did, till we loved? were we not weaned till then?
But sucked on country pleasures, childishly?
Or snorted we in the Seven Sleepers' den?
'Twas so; but this, all pleasures fancies be.
If ever any beauty I did see,
Which I desired, and got, 'twas but a dream of thee.

And now good-morrow to our waking souls,
Which watch not one another out of fear;
For love, all love of other sights controls,
And makes one little room an everywhere.
Let sea-discoverers to new worlds have gone,
Let maps to others, worlds on worlds have shown,
Let us possess one world, each hath one, and is one.

My face in thine eye, thine in mine appears,
And true plain hearts do in the faces rest;
Where can we find two better hemispheres,
Without sharp north, without declining west?
Whatever dies, was not mixed equally;
If our two loves be one, or, thou and I
Love so alike, that none do slacken, none can die.

John Donne (1572 – 1631)

Blessing
for Livvy and Jamie

That your love may be a walled garden
Newly tattered by rain, which comes suddenly
And stutters its few pearls on the lady's mantle

And in this walled garden, which is your love
Lupins spread their fingers, honeysuckling
Moths bear the walls' patterns, goldfinches tap –

Teasels tickle. This for you, who are no ordinary lovers
Who drink rain and mist and above all light
That dances and creeps and hopes

That your love may be wild and rampant
Multiplying like the mysterious foxgloves
Sweet and persistent as mallow

Fire-tipped like phlox
In its fierce dance of reconciliation
And meadowsweet and woodruff

Come to scent the cool halls of your
Marriage. Your love is a walled garden
May season follow season

Scent follow scent
The pattern of love flourish and root itself
Deeper and wider and lay its own seeds

Bluebell and harebell and comfrey and sage:
In the naming of love how sweet it grows
A hundred greening names to your young garden

In its ancient walls. Your love
Is a walled garden, and yet there will be
No name to contain it

Sasha Dugdale

On Marriage

Then Almitra spoke again and said, And what of Marriage, master?
And he answered saying:
You were born together, and together you shall be for evermore.
You shall be together when the white wings of death scatter your days.
Aye, you shall be together even in the silent memory of God.
But let there be spaces in your togetherness.
And let the winds of the heavens dance between you.

Love one another, but make not a bond of love:
Let it rather be a moving sea between the shores of your souls.
Fill each other's cup but drink not from one cup.
Give one another of your bread but eat not from the same loaf.
Sing and dance together and be joyous, but let each one of you be alone,
Even as the strings of the lute are alone though they quiver with the same music.

Give your hearts, but not into each other's keeping.
For only the hand of Life can contain your hearts.
And stand together yet not too near together:
For the pillars of the temple stand apart,
And the oak tree and the cypress grow not in each other's shadow.

Kahlil Gibran (1883 – 1931)

Tree Marriage

In Chota Nagpur and Bengal
the betrothed are tied with threads to
mango trees, they marry the trees
as well as one another, and
the two trees marry each other.
Could we do that some time with oaks
or beeches? This gossamer we
hold each other with, this web
of love and habit is not enough.
In mistrust of heavier ties,
I would like tree-siblings for us,
standing together somewhere, two
trees married with us, lightly, their
fingers barely touching in sleep,
our threads invisible but holding.

William Meredith (1919 – 2007)

A Blessing for Wedding

Today when persimmons ripen
Today when fox-kits come out of their den into snow
Today when the spotted egg releases its wren song
Today when the maple sets down its red leaves
Today when windows keep their promise to open
Today when fire keeps its promise to warm
Today when someone you love has died
    or someone you never met has died
Today when someone you love has been born
    or someone you will not meet has been born
Today when rain leaps to the waiting of roots in their dryness
Today when starlight bends to the roofs of the hungry and tired
Today when someone sits long inside his last sorrow
Today when someone steps into the heat of her first embrace
Today, let day and dark bless you
With binding of seed and rind bless you
With snow-chill and lavender bless you
Let the vow of this day keep itself wildly and wholly
Spoken and silent, surprise you inside your ears
Sleeping and waking, unfold itself inside your eyes
Let its fierceness and tenderness hold you
Let its vastness be undisguised in all your days

Jane Hirshfield

The Present

For the present there is just one moon,
though every level pond gives back another.

But the bright disc shining in the black lagoon,
perceived by astrophysicist and lover,

is milliseconds old. And even that light's
seven minutes older than its source.

And the stars we think we see on moonless nights
are long extinguished. And, of course,

this very moment, as you read this line,
is literally gone before you know it.

Forget the here-and-now. We have no time
but this device of wantonness and wit.

Make me this present then: your hand in mine
and we'll live out our lives in it.

Michael Donaghy (1954 – 2004)

Honeymooners' Ghazal

You teach me the name of each bird, my love,
and I test on my tongue every word, my love.

A young redshank boomerangs in towards shore,
where her water-flute cry can be heard, my love.

At Mull Head's rocky ledge, dark cormorants stand
and survey the white spume churned to cud, my love.

We watch gannets pierce the linen of mist,
pulling fast an invisible cord, my love.

When a sea-fret blows in from the coast then exhales,
once again you're beside me, unblurred my love.

A hooded crow flaps its course into squall
round the cliffs of Deerness, undeterred, my love.

Kittiwakes glide – they trace rings with their wings
and your voice is the air they've stirred, my love.

Kathryn Bevis